BEGINNING TO END

Wax to Crayon

by Bryan Langdo

BELLWETHER MEDIA · MINNEAPOLIS, MN

Blastoff! Readers are carefully developed by literacy experts to build reading stamina and move students toward fluency by combining standards-based content with developmentally appropriate text.

Level 1 provides the most support through repetition of high-frequency words, light text, predictable sentence patterns, and strong visual support.

Level 2 offers early readers a bit more challenge through varied sentences, increased text load, and text-supportive special features.

Level 3 advances early-fluent readers toward fluency through increased text load, less reliance on photos, advancing concepts, longer sentences, and more complex special features.

★ **Blastoff! Universe**

Reading Level

Grade **K**

Grades **1–3**

Grade **4**

This edition first published in 2024 by Bellwether Media, Inc.

No part of this publication may be reproduced in whole or in part without written permission of the publisher. For information regarding permission, write to Bellwether Media, Inc., Attention: Permissions Department, 6012 Blue Circle Drive, Minnetonka, MN 55343.

Library of Congress Cataloging-in-Publication Data

Names: Langdo, Bryan, author.
Title: Wax to crayon / by Bryan Langdo.
Description: Minneapolis : Bellwether Media, Inc., [2024] | Series: Blastoff! readers. Beginning to end | Includes bibliographical references and index. | Audience: Ages 5-8 | Audience: Grades 2-3 | Summary: "Relevant images match informative text in this introduction to how wax is made into crayons. Intended for students in kindergarten through third grade"– Provided by publisher.
Identifiers: LCCN 2023006491 (print) | LCCN 2023006492 (ebook) | ISBN 9798886874266 (library binding) | ISBN 9798886875362 (paperback) | ISBN 9798886876147 (ebook)
Subjects: LCSH: Crayons–Juvenile literature. | Paraffin wax–Juvenile literature.
Classification: LCC TS1268 .L36 2024 (print) | LCC TS1268 (ebook) | DDC 665/.1–dc23/eng/20230302
LC record available at https://lccn.loc.gov/2023006491
LC ebook record available at https://lccn.loc.gov/2023006492

Editor: Elizabeth Neuenfeldt   Designer: Laura Sowers

Printed in the United States of America, North Mankato, MN.

Table of Contents

Start with Wax

Do you know how crayons are made? They are made from wax!

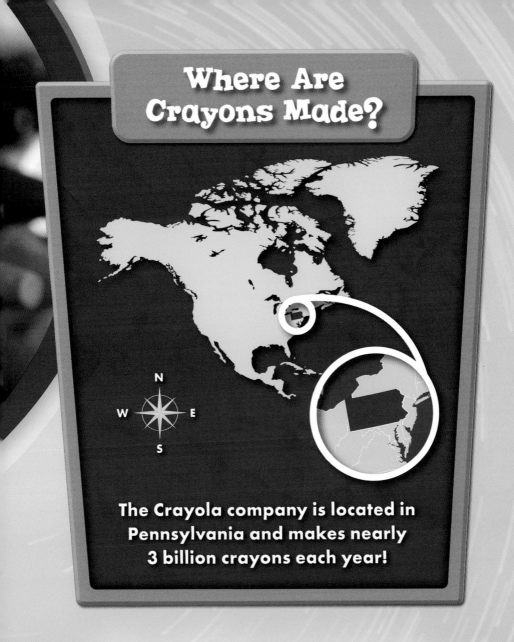

Where Are Crayons Made?

The Crayola company is located in Pennsylvania and makes nearly 3 billion crayons each year!

A special **process** turns the wax into crayons.

crayon factory

GATX 89824

Paraffin wax arrives
at a crayon factory.
The wax is made from oil.

It has no smell or taste.
It is mostly clear.

paraffin wax

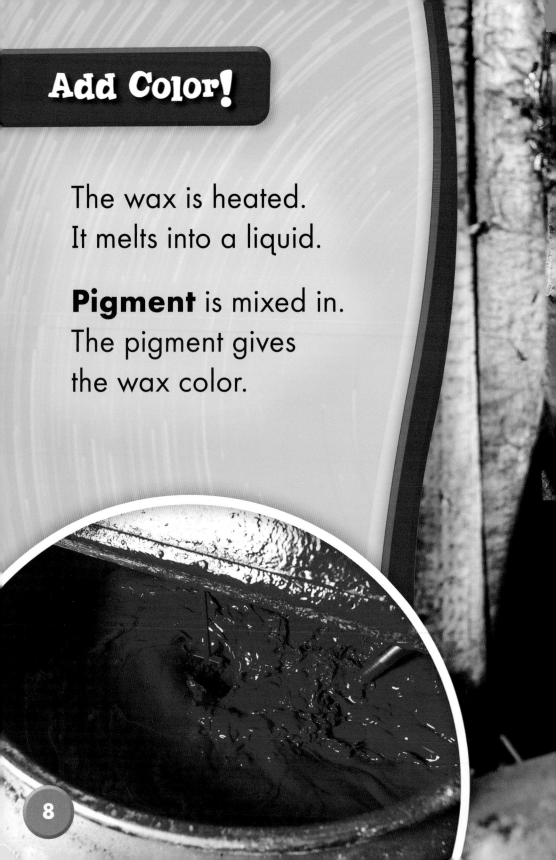

Add Color!

The wax is heated.
It melts into a liquid.

Pigment is mixed in.
The pigment gives
the wax color.

pigment

A Rainbow of Colors

Crayola crayons come in 120 different colors!

rotary machine

The colorful wax is poured into a **rotary machine**.

This machine has a lot of **molds**. The molds are shaped like crayons!

molds

Cold water surrounds the molds. The wax quickly cools. It hardens.

blade

A blade cuts off extra wax.
Then the machine pushes
the crayons out.

The crayons go on a **conveyor**. It brings the crayons to a **labeling machine**.

This machine glues paper labels onto the crayons.

conveyor

CAUTION

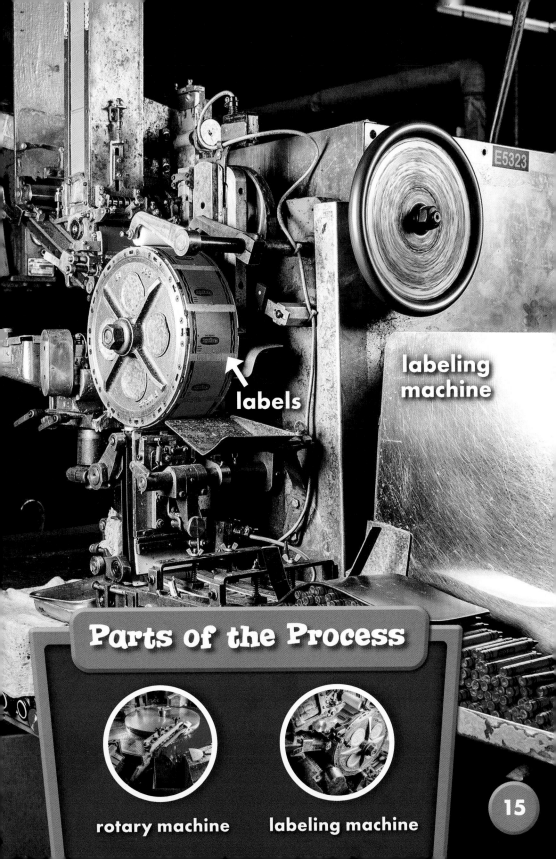

labels

labeling machine

E5323

Parts of the Process

rotary machine

labeling machine

Sorting Crayons

Workers gather the labeled crayons. They sort the crayons by color.

The different colors go into **hoppers**. The hoppers are part of a **packaging machine**.

hoppers

The packaging machine moves the crayons. It sorts the crayons into sets. It pushes the sets into boxes. Then the crayon boxes are sent to stores!

Wax to Crayon

1 paraffin wax
is melted

2 pigment is
mixed in

3 the colorful wax is
poured into molds
to make crayons

4 labels are glued
onto the crayons

5 the crayons are sorted

6 the crayons go
into boxes

Time to Draw!

Crayons come in a lot of colors. Some have glitter. Some even glow in the dark!

Kids everywhere love drawing with crayons!

Glossary

conveyor—a machine with a belt that can move things

hoppers—containers that can unload things

labeling machine—a machine that puts paper labels onto things

molds—open containers in which substances can be shaped

packaging machine—a machine that puts things into boxes or other containers

paraffin wax—a type of wax made from oil

pigment—a colorful powder that can be mixed in to give things color

process—a number of steps taken to reach an end result

rotary machine—a machine with a lot of molds that slowly turns and makes a lot of crayons

To Learn More

AT THE LIBRARY

Biebow, Natascha. *The Crayon Man: The True Story of the Invention of Crayola Crayons*. Boston, Mass.: Houghton Mifflin Harcourt, 2019.

Miller, Derek. *Crayons*. New York, N.Y.: Cavendish Square, 2020.

Toolen, Avery. *From Wax to Crayon*. Minneapolis, Minn.: Bullfrog Books, 2022.

ON THE WEB

FACTSURFER

Factsurfer.com gives you a safe, fun way to find more information.

1. Go to www.factsurfer.com.

2. Enter "wax to crayon" into the search box and click 🔍.

3. Select your book cover to see a list of related content.

Index